GUADALCANAL

by

Wallace B. Black
and
Jean F. Blashfield

CRESTWOOD HOUSE
New York

Maxwell Macmillan Canada
Toronto

Maxwell Macmillan International
New York Oxford Singapore Sydney

Library of Congress Cataloging-in-Publication Data

Black, Wallace B.
    Guadalcanal / by Wallace B. Black and Jean F. Blashfield. — 1st ed.
      p.   cm. — (World War II 50th anniversary series)
    Includes index.
    Summary: Describes the World War II battle between the Japanese and American forces for control of the strategic island of Guadalcanal.
    ISBN 0-89686-560-6
    1. Guadalcanal Island (Solomon Islands), Battle of, 1942-1943—Juvenile literature. [1. Guadalcanal Island (Solomon Islands), Battle of, 1942-1943. 2. World War, 1939-1945—Campaigns—Pacific Area.] I. Blashfield, Jean F. II. Title. III. Series: Black, Wallace B. World War II 50th anniversary series.
D767.98.B54 1992
940.54'26 — dc20

                           91-19902
                           CIP
                           AC

Created and produced by B & B Publishing, Inc.

Picture Credits
Dave Conant - page 11 (map)
National Archives - pages 3, 4, 6, 9, 12, 13, 14, 17, 19, 21, 23, 24, 25, 26, 27, 40, 43, 44, 45 (both)
United States Air Force - pages 39, 41
United States Navy - pages 8, 22, 29, 30, 31, 35, 36, 38

CRESTWOOD HOUSE

Macmillan Publishing Company
866 Third Avenue
New York, NY 10022

Maxwell Macmillan Canada, Inc.
1200 Eglinton Avenue East
Suite 200
Don Mills, Ontario M3C 3N1

Macmillan Publishing Company is part of the Maxwell Communication Group of Companies.

Printed in the United States of America

First Edition

10 9 8 7 6 5 4 3 2 1

CONTENTS

1. Battles in the Pacific — The Road Back 5
2. U.S. Marines Invade Guadalcanal 10
3. Land Battles on Guadalcanal 20
4. Solomon Islands — Battles at Sea 28
5. The Guadalcanal Air Force 37
6. Victory at Last 42

A Closer Look at 45

Glossary 46

Index 47

Chapter 1

BATTLES IN THE PACIFIC — THE ROAD BACK

Following their sneak attack on Pearl Harbor in Hawaii on December 7, 1941, Japanese armed forces conquered and occupied most of the island nations in the western Pacific. They were rapidly advancing and occupying new territory on mainland Asia. Territory in China, Indochina, Thailand, the Malay Peninsula, Hong Kong and Burma fell to their advancing armies. The Japanese navy appeared invincible as it captured one island after another and drove rapidly southward toward Australia — and Guadalcanal.

The Dutch, French and British were easily defeated and their colonies captured. The United States had lost much of its Pacific Fleet. It could do nothing to help stop the onslaught of the Japanese invaders, either on land or at sea.

When the Japanese attacked the Philippine Islands, the American and Filipino armed forces stationed there held out for six months against overwhelming odds. Under the command of General Douglas MacArthur, they bravely fought a losing battle. The U.S. and Filipino forces in the Philippines surrendered to the Japanese on May 6, 1942.

One brief moment of victory for the United States was the successful raid on Tokyo, the capital of Japan. Under the command of Lieutenant Colonel Jimmy Doolittle, a flight of 15 U.S. Army Air Corps B-25 Mitchell bombers attacked Japan. Taking off from the aircraft carrier USS *Hornet,* the

Main street at Guadalcanal headquarters

Tokyo raiders were able to make the Japanese people experience war for the first time. It was a great blow to Japanese pride and a real boost for American morale.

Japanese Advances Continue

With the conquest of the Philippines out of the way, the Japanese forces continued south toward Australia. Their goal was to establish bases to support an invasion of Australia and cut U.S. supply lines to the South Pacific. There was no interference from the sea or the air as they occupied Borneo and a large part of the huge island of New Guinea.

In early May 1942 a huge fleet of Japanese warships and transports headed toward Australia. Their goal was to invade and capture Port Moresby in the part of New Guinea they didn't control. They also planned to set up bases on Guadalcanal in the Solomon Islands. But the U.S. Navy learned of these plans and sent a major naval force to stop the Japanese advance.

After capturing Wake Island, a U.S. possession in the Pacific Ocean, Japanese troops honor fallen comrades.

Flattop Against Flattop

As the Battle of the Coral Sea started just to the northeast of Australia, the Japanese navy drew first blood. Planes from a Japanese aircraft carrier, also called a flattop, sank two American ships. At the same time planes from U.S. carriers scored a major victory of their own. They located part of a Japanese force approaching New Guinea and successfully attacked and sank the Japanese aircraft carrier *Shoho.* This was the first major victory by U.S. Navy aircraft in the war.

Then came the main action in the Coral Sea. At no time did ships of either navy come in sight of each other. Instead their fighters, dive-bombers and torpedo-bombers went into action. The battle ended with major damage to both fleets. The United States lost the carrier *Lexington,* which was sunk after repeated bombing and torpedo attacks. The carrier *Yorktown* was also damaged.

At the same time, the giant Japanese carrier *Shokaku* was seriously damaged. The Japanese called off the Port Moresby invasion. All of the Japanese units withdrew to the north, leaving the American fleet in control of the Coral Sea. In spite of heavy losses, it was a victory for the U.S. Pacific Fleet.

The Battle of Midway

Just a few weeks later another great air and sea battle took place. Under the command of Japanese Admiral Isoroku Yamamoto, another giant Japanese force was ready to attack. Its goal was to capture Midway Island north of Hawaii.

The Japanese force was made up of a huge fleet of troopships, defending warships and four aircraft carriers. They far outnumbered the U.S. Pacific Fleet that was preparing to defend Midway.

Success of this mission would have given the Japanese control of the western Pacific Ocean from Alaska in the

Sailors fought fires on the aircraft carrier USS Yorktown *during the Battle of the Coral Sea. The USS* Lexington, *in the background, was sunk later that day.*

north to Australia in the south and all of the Pacific Ocean and lands west of Hawaii. It had to be stopped. Again a valiant U.S. naval force, spearheaded by three aircraft carriers, would defeat a larger and more powerful Japanese naval force.

The battle started on June 4, 1942, when Japanese aircraft attacked Midway. This attack did considerable damage but was driven off. The next day continuous battles between aircraft from the opposing flattops of both sides took place. Although the *Lexington* was sunk, the Japanese lost all four of their giant flattops along with all the aircraft and crews.

Victorious at Midway but still badly prepared for all-out war, the United States and its allies hastened to prepare for the next Japanese attacks.

Marines landing at Guadalcanal were surprised to find no Japanese troops contesting the landings.

Chapter 2

U.S. MARINES INVADE GUADALCANAL

The Japanese navy was staggering after the beating it took at Midway and the failure of its Coral Sea campaign. The U.S. Pacific Fleet was happy but also licking its wounds. However, the entire might of the Japanese army was intact and ready to continue its conquests. And the Japanese navy, despite its losses, was still far larger and better equipped than the U.S. Navy in the Pacific.

The Japanese were intent on controlling all of the Pacific Ocean west of the Hawaiian Islands. Japanese Premier Hideki Tojo and Admiral Yamamoto kept their losses at Midway a secret from the Japanese people. They ordered further expansion in the area to the east and south of New Guinea.

When the Japanese task force headed for the Coral Sea, their army troops first occupied Tulagi Island. This is a small island in the center of the Solomon Islands. Landings on the nearby larger island called Guadalcanal followed. Over 2,000 Japanese troops occupied the northeast coast of that island and began building an airstrip.

U.S. Naval Intelligence was aware of these activities. Although not at all ready for another major sea battle, the U.S. high command decided that the Japanese advances in the Solomons must be stopped. In July 1942, under the command of Vice Admiral Robert Ghormley, an invasion task force was formed. Its goal was to occupy Guadalcanal and to drive the Japanese from the Solomon Islands.

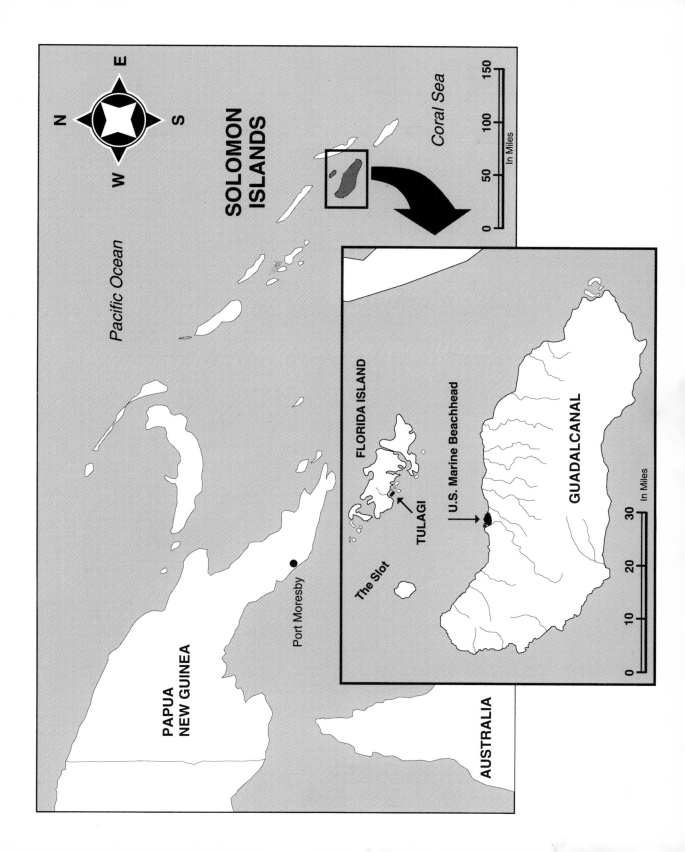

The Solomons are located in the South Pacific Ocean north of Australia. They are a chain of volcanic islands about 1,500 miles long, made up of several large islands and numerous smaller ones. The Japanese continued their efforts to fortify the Solomon Islands of Guadalcanal and Tulagi. They planned to use bases there for attacks on Australia and the U.S. supply lines to the South Pacific.

The Solomon Islands

At the beginning of World War II the Solomon Islands were controlled by Great Britain. As the Japanese invaders moved southward in the spring of 1942 the British left.

Eight large islands in two parallel lines make up the Solomon Islands. Guadalcanal at the south end is one of the largest and most mountainous. The long channel between the groups of islands was called "the slot." Time and time again Japanese naval forces would sail down the slot to attack U.S. forces and reinforce their troops on Guadalcanal.

Natives helped the U.S. Marines by acting as coastwatchers and guides.

Landing craft loaded with marines head for shore at Guadalcanal.

The United States knew very little about Guadalcanal. The few maps that were available carried little information of military value. Former British plantation owners, some of whom were still hiding out on the islands, offered additional help. Many of these planters and Solomon Islands natives served as "coastwatchers" on the islands and secretly kept the U.S. forces informed of enemy ground and air activity.

Operation Watchtower

In the early morning hours of August 7, 1942, 19,000 nervous young American marines were on board the ships of a huge invasion fleet. They had arrived at Skylark Channel near Guadalcanal and tiny Tulagi Island.

These well-trained and battle-ready marines were the 1st Marine Division under the command of Major General Alexander A. (Archie) Vandegrift. They were part of an amphibious task force, made up of some 80 warships, transports and cargo ships. This force was about to undertake Operation Watchtower. It was America's first major amphibious landing on an enemy-held island in World War II.

Supporting the invasion fleet was a naval task force under the command of Rear Admiral Frank J. Fletcher. It was made up of three aircraft carriers — *Saratoga, Enterprise* and *Wasp* — with approximately 250 aircraft. The flattops were supported by a battleship, 6 cruisers and 16 destroyers. An aerial task force, made up of land-based aircraft from islands to the south, was also available. These 292 fighters and bombers would fly to Guadalcanal as soon as the airfield being built there was ready.

The Landings — Tulagi Island

Shortly after 6:00 A.M. on August 7, fighters and dive-bombers from the aircraft carrier *Wasp* began strafing and bombing Tulagi Island. At the same time a destroyer and several cruisers began pumping shells from their deck guns into enemy caves and bunkers.

Abandoning their landing craft, marines waded ashore at Tulagi Island.

Several scouting parties scrambled ashore at 7:40 A.M. The main attacking body of Marine Raiders followed at 8:00 A.M. But their landing craft got stuck on heavy coral reefs and the men had to struggle ashore in shoulder-deep water. No shots were fired and no enemy was in sight.

However, the Japanese troops were firmly entrenched in their caves on Tulagi and neighboring islands. Soon they started shooting. Fighting went on for the next two days as the "leathernecks," as the marines were called, cleaned up one pocket of Japanese defenders after another. All enemy resistance on Tulagi ended on August 9. About 600 of the enemy were killed, escaped or were captured. U.S. casualties, mostly wounded, were fewer than 250.

Guadalcanal — The First Day

The scene was somewhat different on Guadalcanal that first morning. Without accurate maps or information concerning the enemy, the landing force commander, General Vandegrift, was not sure what the marines would find. They loaded into their landing craft and headed for Red Beach near Lunga Point on the northeast shore of Guadalcanal.

There was no sign of the enemy. But the first marines to land set up defensive positions to fight off possible attacks. By midday 5,000 men and hundreds of boatloads of supplies had landed. Scouting parties searched for the enemy and found none.

But the Japanese headquarters in Rabaul, located on New Britain Island, had been notified by radio of the invading forces. They ordered air strikes immediately. Twice that day Japanese bombers attacked. Warned in advance by British and native coastwatchers, the U.S. forces were ready. Only one ship was struck by a bomb and no attacks were made on the troops or supplies that had been landed. And several Japanese bombers were shot down.

As night fell on that first day there was still no sign of

the enemy. All units that had come ashore carefully settled down for the night. Nervous, inexperienced troops were on guard against the unseen enemy. They fired at the slightest movement they saw during the hours of darkness. There were some Americans wounded, perhaps from friendly fire. There was still no confirmed contact with a Japanese force of any size.

Guadalcanal — The Second Day

The marines' original objective was a point of high ground several miles inland named Mount Austen. Upon landing, the marines were blocked from reaching this goal by dense jungle. The terrain was rough, the river banks too steep and the streams too deep. General Vandegrift immediately changed plans and the objective became the Japanese airfield.

Upon reaching what would later become Henderson Field, the marines found that the Japanese troops had left in panic. Warm food was on tables in the mess halls. Large supplies of food, ammunition and equipment were found in perfect condition. The enemy had made no attempt to destroy their supplies before fleeing.

When the American forces captured the airfield, they named it Henderson Field after Major Loften Henderson, a marine squadron leader who was killed earlier during the Battle of Midway. The second day was spent reinforcing Red Beach and securing the airfield. Still with no opposition, the marines moved farther inland.

Although a few individual enemy soldiers had been encountered, there was still no ground action. But again Japanese bombers attacked. About 40 twin-engine torpedo planes arrived and attacked the naval forces lying offshore in Skylark Channel. The destroyer USS *Jarvis* was hit and it sank with all hands on board. The transport *Elliot* was set afire when an enemy plane crashed into it. This ship was abandoned and destroyed.

In addition to the sinking of two ships, the Japanese gained valuable intelligence. Their returning bombers furnished information on the location of American transports and warships. A Japanese task force was already speeding down the slot to attack the U.S. ships and shell the Guadalcanal landing force.

As the second day ended, the marines on Guadalcanal were still searching for the enemy. Heavily bombed two days in a row, they nervously awaited the first ground battles. They expected more aerial bombardment and the arrival of enemy reinforcements and warships attacking by sea.

Guadalcanal — The Third Day

Day three was filled with bad news. During the previous night a defending force of five U.S. cruisers had been attacked and destroyed near Savo Island. Surprised by a superior Japanese force at the north end of Skylark Channel, four cruisers were set ablaze and sank. The U.S. naval force protecting the transports that were anchored off Guadalcanal no longer existed. After that night, August 8, Skylark Channel was named Ironbottom Sound because of the large number of ships sunk there.

Marines digging foxholes and fortifications around Henderson Field

To make matters worse, Admiral Fletcher, fearing additional attacks from Japanese naval forces and land-based and carrier aircraft, ordered the withdrawal of the entire invasion fleet. By the afternoon of August 9 further landings were cancelled and all ships had left. The marine forces on Guadalcanal and Tulagi were on their own. Less than half of the invading force and their supplies had been landed.

In addition, the ground-based aircraft that had been promised for air support would not arrive at Henderson Field for another two weeks. And no one knew when the departing transports and cargo ships would return.

The Marines Dig In

The marines immediately expanded Red Beach about two miles east, west and inland. This small area included Henderson Field. About 6,000 men and mountains of supplies had been landed there. Another 2,000 men and a limited amount of equipment had been landed on Tulagi. The rest of the 70-mile-long Guadalcanal Island was controlled by the original Japanese force of 2,000 men plus reinforcements that were continually arriving.

The marines had enough food for only thirty days and ammunition for about three days of heavy fighting. In addition, General Vandegrift's forces lacked heavy equipment, barbed wire, tanks, gasoline, ammunition for the big guns and other supplies.

By the third day the U.S. lines extended about five miles along the beach and inland about two miles. This small area was to be all the marines would control on Guadalcanal for the next four months.

Beach defenses were immediately established. Artillery units dug in and patrols went out along the inland borders of the landing area. They were still searching for Japanese defenders. General Vandegrift established a command post. Each unit of marines dug foxholes, set up fortified encampments and prepared to repel enemy attacks. Mountains of

Marines on guard in a camouflaged jungle foxhole

supplies were still being moved inland from the beach.

Marine labor battalions went to work on the unfinished airfield and by August 11 it was ready to receive light aircraft. But none came. More than a week would pass before the first planes arrived. It would be several months before the strip could be used for heavy bombers and all-weather flight operations.

Even though they were short of supplies and equipment, the leathernecks were ready to fight. Young and nervous, the average marines on Guadalcanal were about 20 years old. Well-trained in the Marine Corps tradition and with superb leadership, they prepared to fight and to meet the enemy whenever and wherever they attacked.

Chapter 3

LAND BATTLES ON GUADALCANAL

Guadalcanal is a hot and humid tropical island that gets more than 120 inches of rainfall per year. The temperature soars into the 90° Fahrenheit levels. Most of the island has high, volcanic mountains. But the low-lying coastal areas occupied by the American marines were overgrown with heavy jungle.

The island was infested with insects, alligators and other wildlife. Both U.S. and Japanese soldiers were victims of malaria and dengue fever carried by mosquitoes. Constant battle, the jungle, rain, mud, insects and disease made life miserable for everyone on both sides.

During the first two weeks on Guadalcanal the marines saw little action. They were busy building their defenses and completing Henderson Field. They made no major attacks against the Japanese. Contact was limited to a few skirmishes with the enemy by marine patrols.

Finally, on August 19, one patrol ran into a small but well-armed Japanese force that wore fresh battle gear. General Vandegrift then knew that Japanese reinforcements had been landed and were ready for battle. All marine units were placed on alert.

The Ichiki Battle

A detachment of 2,000 crack Japanese troops under the command of Colonel Kyono Ichiki had landed. An overconfident Colonel Ichiki, not waiting for additional artillery support, attacked the eastern defenses of Red Beach.

Believing that heavy bombing and naval bombardment

This picture of a Japanese machine gun crew in dress uniforms was found in the belongings of a dead Japanese soldier.

had weakened the marines, the Japanese launched a full-scale attack. In predawn darkness they charged across sandbars at the mouth of the Tenaru River. Their goal was to breach the U.S. lines and recapture Henderson Field. But the leathernecks were ready and waiting.

The Japanese attacked with machine guns and flame-throwers, their flags waving and bugles blaring. But the U.S. Marines were dug into carefully concealed positions on the west bank of the Tenaru. As the Japanese charge reached midstream the marines opened fire.

The entire Ichiki detachment of some 2,000 men was stopped cold. Intense fire from rifles, machine guns and artillery firing canister shells (shells loaded with hundreds of pellets) mowed down the attackers. More marines attacked the invaders from inland. U.S. tanks added to the fire power and the battle was soon over. More than 900 Japanese died while U.S. casualties were less than 100. The Battle of the Tenaru had ended in disaster for the Japanese. Colonel Ichiki, disgraced by the defeat, committed *hari-kari* (suicide).

The Tokyo Express

Following this disaster the Japanese made every effort to bring more reinforcements to Guadalcanal. Japanese destroyers and cruisers traveling at night were nicknamed the Tokyo Express. They raced down the Solomon Islands slot at night to deliver supplies and reinforcements. By both night and day, warships and aircraft would bombard Henderson Field and the five-mile patch of jungle that had been claimed by the U.S. Marines.

Starting their missions at dusk at a point about 200 miles north of Guadalcanal, the Tokyo Express warships would begin their run. Under cover of darkness they would unload their cargo of troops and supplies at about 2:00 A.M. They would fire a few broadsides toward Henderson Field and then head back north. Marine and navy pilots tried to intercept the express just as the ships started their high-speed missions or as they returned to their bases at dawn.

U.S. Navy SBD dive-bomber flying over the wreckage of two Japanese ships destroyed off Guadalcanal

Stripped for action, a marine mans a heavy machine gun.

Battle of Bloody Ridge

The high command in Tokyo finally realized that the marines on Guadalcanal were a force to be reckoned with. They called off action on other fronts and gave their full attention to driving the Americans from Guadalcanal. A force of over 6,000 battle-hardened troops under the command of Major General Kiyotaje Kawaguchi prepared to land at both ends of the patch of jungle held by the Americans. Constant aerial and naval bombardment pounded the marines and the airfield for days before the landings. By September 11 the Kawaguchi raiders were in position to charge ashore.

Kawaguchi's troops landed at the east end of the marines' small patch of land. But General Vandegrift anticipated this action. He had Lieutenant Colonel Merritt A. Edson bring a force of marine paratroopers over from Tulagi to attack the unsuspecting Japanese as they landed. The surprise was complete. The marine attackers captured or destroyed Japanese supplies and equipment and drove the Japanese landing force into the jungle. This action weakened and delayed Kawaguchi's plan of attack.

Finally the Japanese had landed in force at both ends of the beach. General Vandegrift immediately reinforced the perimeter on all four sides. Defensive positions were hastily dug along a ridge just south of Henderson Field. All armor and artillery were positioned so that any side of the rectangle could be defended.

On the morning of September 12, Kawaguchi ordered simultaneous attacks from the east, west and south. Colonel Edson and his paratroopers took up position on the ridge to the south of the airfield — and just in time. At midmorning the Japanese attacked Edson's Ridge. The marines on the ridge were badly outnumbered and were driven back toward the airfield. Enemy air raids and naval bombardment made the situation even worse.

Finally, in the midst of Japanese attacks, Edson was reinforced by another battalion of marines moving inland from the beach. Time and time again they drove the Kawaguchi forces back. Twelve times the enemy charged and twelve times they were forced to retreat. Small units of Japanese even fought their way to the airstrip and General Vandegrift's headquarters before being mowed down. The superb fighting spirit and skill of the marine defenders saved the day. By the end of September 14 as the fighting ended, Edson's Ridge had become known as "Bloody Ridge."

Highly maneuverable marine and army light tanks played a key role in fighting off the Japanese on Guadalcanal.

U.S. Marines fording a jungle stream

The Sendai Campaign

Following the Battle of Bloody Ridge both sides strengthened their positions and brought in reinforcements. Admiral Richard K. Turner successfully brought a group of transports through a naval battle in the eastern Solomons to land a force of 4,000 marines. Hundreds of trucks, artillery pieces, ammunition, gasoline and food were landed. The battle-weary troops were relieved and refreshed. Edson's paratroopers and other battered and malaria-ridden troops were able to leave the island.

Through the early weeks of October both sides continued to build their forces. By October 15 the American troop strength had increased to 22,000. The Japanese force increased to 23,000.

Vandegrift, using his reinforcements and new equipment, stretched his front line on the beach another three miles to the west. There he set up a defensive position on the Matanikau River like the one to the east on the Tenaru. There were now a dozen divisions in position around the perimeter, supported by artillery, tanks and, finally, an ever-increasing air force.

As mid-October approached Vandegrift was ready for another major Japanese attack. U.S. Navy, Marine and Army aircraft were being flown into Guadalcanal in a steady stream. But just as quickly they were destroyed by gunfire and aerial bombardment and in aerial combat. Finally, on October 13, continuous bombardment around the clock almost put Henderson Field out of commission for good. But by the next morning repair crews had patched up bomb holes in the runways. Ground crews repaired damaged aircraft. The Cactus Air Force, named after cactus-like jungle plants of the Solomon Islands, was back in business.

Meanwhile, under the command of Lieutenant General Haruyoshi Hyakutake, the well-trained Japanese Sendai Division arrived on Guadalcanal. By October 20 they were ready to attack. The Sendai made minor thrusts at various points along the perimeter, but their first major attack came from the west. The screaming Japanese tried to charge across the Matanikau River and attack Henderson Field. This effort resulted in the slaughter of most of the Japanese force on the river sandbars.

Three days later a Japanese tank force tried to breach the defenses to the east. Marine artillery blasted the tanks and the Japanese infantry that followed behind. This attack also failed.

A Japanese heavy tank disabled by U.S. Marine anti-tank gunners

Japanese dead lie on the beach following a hard-fought battle near the Tenaru River.

The Sendai regiment finally launched three attacks from inland points over the ridge toward the heavily defended airstrip. These attacks, on October 24 and 25, earned the name the Battle for Henderson Field. If the Japanese attacks had been made simultaneously instead of separately the outcome might have been different. General Hyakutake's final attack on Henderson Field was stopped.

The unwavering leathernecks, reinforced by newly arrived U.S. Army battalions, were more than a match for the Sendai. The beaten and broken Japanese attackers retreated helter-skelter into the jungle. At no time after this defeat were the Japanese on Guadalcanal able to launch a major offensive in the face of growing U.S. military strength.

Chapter 4

SOLOMON ISLANDS — BATTLES AT SEA

From their first landing on Red Beach on Guadalcanal on August 7, 1942, until the final withdrawal of Japanese troops during February 1943, the U.S. Marines fought valiantly. But the victorious outcome would have been impossible without the support of the U.S. Pacific Fleet. Battered in one battle after another against the Japanese navy, U.S. naval forces gave the final measure of support that made victory on Guadalcanal possible.

In July 1942 the U.S. Navy high command knew that the Japanese had landed in force on Guadalcanal. They had to be stopped. The Pacific Fleet performed admirably, finally landing more than 19,000 marines and large quantities of supplies on the island. During the initial landings only one destroyer and one transport were lost to enemy action. It was a small price to pay for a successful landing. But this situation soon changed.

Disaster at Savo Island

Skylark Channel to the northeast of Guadalcanal earned its nickname of Ironbottom Sound on the night of August 8, 1942. At midnight that night a strong fleet of Japanese warships sped down the slot toward Guadalcanal. Seven cruisers and accompanying destroyers planned to attack and destroy the American troop transports and defending warships at Guadalcanal.

Unaware of the approaching Japanese force, U.S. cruisers and destroyers took positions in Ironbottom Sound. They were to protect the unarmed transports from possible

U.S. Marines launched from a U.S. Navy cruiser in inflatable landing craft for an attack on Guadalcanal.

attack. At about 1:00 A.M. Japanese scout planes were heard overhead, but no one on the American ships spotted the approaching Japanese fleet.

Slipping past an American destroyer, the Japanese force moved swiftly around Savo Island. A short time later the Japanese spotted the U.S. cruisers. The Australian cruiser *Canberra* was hit immediately by high explosive shells and began to sink. The USS *Chicago* was also hit and limped from the battle.

This engagement lasted only ten minutes. Afterward the Japanese cruisers swung to the north. The remaining U.S. warships were now aware of the attack. However, radio communications between them failed. Faulty star shells that failed to light the scene left them in the dark. The approaching Japanese, unseen by the Americans, finally lit their targets with searchlights and opened fire.

The U.S. cruisers *Vincennes, Quincy* and *Astoria* were hit repeatedly by shells and torpedoes from the superior Japanese force. Only the lead Japanese cruiser *Chokai* was damaged by U.S. guns. In this sea battle near Savo Island, four U.S. cruisers had been sunk and one was badly damaged. Some 1,270 Americans were dead and 709 wounded. It was a disaster for the U.S. Navy and a great victory for the Japanese.

However, fearing the presence of U.S. aircraft carriers and their fighters and bombers, the Japanese failed to follow up on their success. As a result, the helpless U.S. troop transports were left unharmed. The attackers turned and sailed northward. They left the scene victorious, but their victory was not complete.

Sea Battles in the Eastern Solomons

At the same time that the Savo Island disaster was taking place, Admiral Frank Fletcher, commanding the U.S. naval forces in the Solomons, decided to withdraw. As the warships left, the transports, many still loaded with troops and supplies, also had to leave. On August 9 the fleet steamed to the south to replenish fuel and ammunition supplies. It also left to avoid combat with Japanese aircraft carriers that might be entering the battle.

For the next two weeks the only real naval attacks in the Solomons were by the Japanese. Almost every night cruisers and destroyers bombarded Henderson Field and the

Navy gunners grab a sandwich while manning an anti-aircraft gun.

The U.S. troop carrier President Coolidge *struck a floating mine near Guadalcanal. The ship was deliberately run aground to keep it from sinking. Over 3,000 troops were able to get safely ashore.*

entrenched marines. U.S. naval activity was limited to small-scale efforts at delivering reinforcements and supplies. Without an air force and deserted by the navy, the marine defenders could only return fire with shore-based guns which had little effect.

But then, to the north of the Solomons, U.S. scouting flights learned that a giant Japanese fleet was gathering. The enemy was preparing to drive the U.S. Marines from Guadalcanal. By this time Fletcher had resupplied his fleet and was cruising about 150 miles south of the Solomons to wait for the Japanese to launch an attack. Receiving faulty information that the Japanese fleet was still far to the north, Fletcher sent the carrier USS *Wasp*, several cruisers and seven destroyers south toward Australia to refuel. To his dismay he then learned that a force of three Japanese flattops and a large supporting force was only 200 miles to the north.

Carrier Forces Attack

Although weakened by the absence of the *Wasp*, Fletcher ordered the *Enterprise* to find the enemy and attack. During a dawn search on August 24 nothing was sighted. But later that morning reports were received of a Japanese aircraft carrier and a large number of supporting warships approaching at full speed.

More aircraft were ordered into the air to locate the enemy. By late afternoon the Japanese aircraft carriers *Shokaku* and *Zuikaku* and about 18 other ships were located just 180 miles to the north. Following close behind this carrier group was a huge invasion force that included a number of large troop transports. The Japanese were on their way to reclaim Guadalcanal.

Torpedo-bombers and dive-bombers from the *Enterprise* attacked the Japanese carrier force immediately. Planes from the recently arrived flattop *Saratoga* also joined in the attack. At the same time a large group of Japanese Kate bombers protected by Zero fighters was encountered as they approached the *Enterprise*. Planes of both sides fought through skies filled with flak (anti-aircraft fire) and defending fighters. Bombs struck ships of both sides and planes went down in flames.

Guadalcanal came under attack from carrier aircraft as the Japanese troop carriers drew closer. Marine fighters from Henderson Field engaged the enemy and shot down about a dozen attacking bombers. Three U.S. fighters were lost. The next morning marine bombers and fighters located the invasion force of four Japanese transports and supporting warships. One large transport and a cruiser were hit by bombs in this attack.

When the score was tallied after this short battle between carriers, the Japanese had lost almost 100 aircraft. In addition the aircraft carrier *Ryujo* had been sunk and four other ships damaged. Faced with continuing attacks from both U.S. carriers and land-based planes from Guadalcanal the Japanese warships and transports turned away and headed back north.

On the U.S. side the *Enterprise* had been damaged and dozens of aircraft had been lost. But all in all, the U.S. Navy had scored a major victory in the Battle of the Eastern Solomons.

Sea Battles a Deciding Factor

Following the Battle of the Eastern Solomons there were no major battles between opposing naval forces until October 11. However, the Japanese were kept very busy in other ways.

After August 20 there were always marine and navy aircraft at Henderson Field. They were used to attack any Japanese reinforcements that attempted to land during the day. As a result, the Japanese continued to run the Tokyo Express at night with particular success. A Japanese submarine fleet concentrated its activities to the south of Guadalcanal near the American carriers. Its assignment was to disrupt supply lines and prevent reinforcements from reaching Guadalcanal.

In mid-September, Japanese submarines torpedoed and sank the giant flattop USS *Wasp* and a destroyer. The new battleship *North Carolina* was damaged. However, the fleet of U.S. transports and other vessels they were protecting made it through to Guadalcanal unharmed.

Cape Esperance and
The Santa Cruz Islands

On the night of October 11, 1942, the first major naval battle close to Guadalcanal since the disaster at Savo Island took place. American forces learned that a Tokyo Express consisting of a small cruiser force was heading down the slot that night. They took up station at Cape Esperance at the northwestern tip of Guadalcanal. What followed was the Savo Island disaster in reverse.

Japanese Rear Admiral Aritomo Goto commanded three heavy cruisers and two destroyers. Their mission was to land reinforcements and supplies and to bombard Henderson Field. As Goto's force approached Savo Island, Rear Admiral Norman Scott, with a superior force of heavy cruisers and destroyers, made a successful surprise attack on the express. Admiral Goto was killed and one heavy cruiser and a destroyer were sunk. The remaining force immediately turned and fled north.

Two weeks later the second major battle between aircraft carrier battle groups took place near the Santa Cruz Islands to the southeast of the Solomons. A vastly superior Japanese force led by four aircraft carriers tangled with a much smaller American force led by two U.S. flattops, the *Hornet* and the *Enterprise.*

Japanese aircraft and ground troops heavily pounded Henderson Field and its defenders throughout October. The large carrier group furnished air cover for an invasion force that was supposed to land after Henderson Field had been captured. But U.S. forces kept control of the airfield and drove off the attacking Japanese transports. Before the Japanese carrier group could withdraw, it was attacked by the American flattops under the command of Admiral Thomas C. Kincaid.

When the losses were added up the American carrier force had been defeated. The *Hornet* was sunk and the *Enterprise* damaged. Two destroyers were also sunk and a

While escorting a convoy of U.S. troopships the USS Wasp *was badly damaged by Japanese planes. In spite of heroic efforts by its crew to save it, the ship sank.*

battleship and a cruiser were damaged. But the important result was that the Japanese had lost more than 100 planes and pilots. Now short of experienced pilots, it became impossible for the Japanese carriers to help out in the final battles for Guadalcanal.

The Battle of Guadalcanal

The final sea battle in the fight for control of Guadalcanal started on the night of November 12, 1942. A strong Japanese force under the command of Admiral Horoaki Abe raced down the slot and into Ironbottom Sound. Their mission was to bombard and destroy Henderson Field. They were met by a cruiser and destroyer force under the command of Rear Admiral Daniel J. Callaghan. In the battle that followed Admiral Callaghan was killed and two American light cruisers and four destroyers were sunk.

But even in death and in spite of great ship losses, Admiral Callaghan was victorious. His force had turned away the Japanese fleet and prevented it from bombarding Henderson Field. The enemy lost two destroyers and the battleship *Hiei* was damaged and then destroyed by planes from Henderson Field.

The next night, unopposed except by PT (patrol torpedo) boats, a smaller Japanese naval force succeeded in shelling the airstrip but not enough to put it out of commission. Later that day planes from the *Enterprise* and from Henderson Field successfully attacked Japanese naval forces in the area.

The U.S. Navy in the South Pacific suffered greatly in the sea battles for Guadalcanal. In only four months dozens of ships were lost and thousands of sailors and airmen died. But as the *Enterprise* retired from the scene of action in November, it did so proudly. Damaged and repaired and damaged and repaired again, it was the only working U.S. carrier left in the Pacific.

But the U.S. Navy's South Pacific Fleet had held the Japanese navy at bay. The navy's army — the U.S. Marine Corps — was able to continue in their conquest of Guadalcanal.

The five Sullivan brothers all served on one cruiser, the USS Juneau. *All five were killed when their ship was sunk during the Battle of Guadalcanal.*

Chapter 5

THE GUADALCANAL AIR FORCE

When the U.S. Marines charged ashore at Guadalcanal on August 7, 1942, they captured the enemy airfield and named it Henderson Field. The first U.S. aircraft landed two weeks later and the so-called Cactus Air Force was born.

Deserted by the U.S. Navy on August 9, the marines on Guadalcanal were without air cover for almost two weeks. They were bombarded daily by Japanese bombers and warships. So when 32 marine aircraft landed at Henderson Field on August 20 they were a welcome sight. Army air corps and navy planes landed a few days later.

The Cactus Air Force

The Marine Air Corps was responsible for the air defense of the island. But that task was easier said than done. Aircraft were always in short supply. Every combat-ready plane in the South Pacific that could land on the short, muddy, bomb-cratered runway at Guadalcanal was brought in. Planes of the army air corps and carrier-based navy fighters and bombers were welcome and put to good use.

The pilots and ground crew stationed there were from the marines, army air corps and navy. They were a rugged bunch. Living in tents they soon became tired, filthy and sick as they fought the tropical rains and the daily bombings in the surrounding cactus-filled jungle from which they derived their name.

Their planes were bombed and destroyed or damaged on the ground. They were damaged by gunfire in aerial combat against the Japanese. There were constant shortages of gasoline, bombs and ammunition. But this ragtag group of pilots that called themselves the Cactus Air Force was always ready for a fight.

Henderson Field was bombed and repaired almost daily. Filled with bomb craters one day, the field was fixed by the marine labor battalions by the next morning. Its surface was covered with special corrugated metal strips so that it could be used in all kinds of weather.

Carrier Aircraft in Action

Someone said that if the navy hadn't lost so many aircraft carriers, Guadalcanal wouldn't have had an air force. Many navy fighters, bombers and torpedo planes had their aircraft carriers sunk from beneath them. The nearest airfield for these homeless aircraft was Henderson Field. Those pilots who didn't run out of gas and ditch their aircraft in the ocean landed at that field. They were immediately drafted into the Cactus Air Force.

A navy dive-bomber taking off from a carrier. Many carrier aircraft were made a part of the Guadalcanal air force.

Marine dive-bombers and light reconnaissance aircraft at Henderson Field

The U.S. flattops were always outnumbered by the Japanese. And the cost in U.S. aircraft carriers was great. The gallant USS *Enterprise* was damaged again and again. The carriers *Wasp* and *Hornet* were both sunk. But at battle's end the hundreds of brave navy pilots flying Wildcat fighters, Dauntless dive-bombers and Avenger torpedo planes were always victorious over the Japanese Zeros, Vals, Kates and other enemy aircraft.

In both the Battle of the Eastern Solomons and the Battle of Santa Cruz the Japanese lost hundreds of planes and pilots to the skill of superior U.S. Navy pilots. As a result of the valiant efforts of the American carriers and their pilots, the Japanese carrier force was not seen in action again until 1944.

The Aces of Guadalcanal

In air force language an ace is a pilot who has successfully shot down five enemy aircraft. The air battles over Guadalcanal made many aces.

On August 20, 1942, Marine Major John L. Smith led the first flights of marine Wildcats to Henderson Field. They went to work on the Japanese raiders the next day and Smith shot down his first Zero fighter. On August 30 Major Smith and his squadron, flying stubby, battleship-gray Wildcat F4F fighters shot down over a dozen Japanese planes. Smith accounted for four. The first high-scoring ace of World War II, Major Smith shot down 19 enemy aircraft and was awarded the Medal of Honor.

One of Smith's squadron mates, Lieutenant Marion Carl, was also an ace. After scoring heavily at Midway, Carl added a dozen or more kills to his record over Guadalcanal. When relieved, Smith's squadron had shot down more than 100 Japanese fighters and bombers. The Cactus Air Force shot down five Japanese planes for every U.S. plane lost.

This landing craft was converted into a mini-aircraft carrier to handle light aircraft for artillery spotting and other aerial reconnaissance.

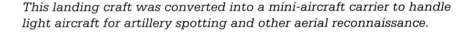

As the Japanese were being pushed off the island, Army Air Force B-25 Mitchell bombers were able to use the improved Henderson Field.

October saw the birth of two more outstanding aces — Captain Joseph J. Foss (later, governor of South Dakota) and his fellow pilot, Lieutenant Colonel Harold W. "Indian Joe" Bauer. Joe Foss went on to become one of the leading aces of World War II. "Indian Joe" Bauer was lost in combat over Guadalcanal after racking up an impressive number of kills. These great aces were among the many brave pilots who helped lead the U.S. Marines to victory on Guadalcanal.

Chapter 6

VICTORY AT LAST

In November 1942, following major defeats of the Japanese on land, sea and in the air, the end of the Guadalcanal campaign was in sight. Although about 23,000 Japanese troops still remained on the island, they were completely disorganized. The American forces had about the same number of marines and army troops. Small battles and firefights continued daily, but now the Americans and not the Japanese were on the offensive.

On November 12 the Japanese bombed and shelled Henderson Field. They were preparing the way for a convoy of a dozen Japanese transports that was approaching Guadalcanal. These transports carried 15,000 troops of the Japanese 38th Division. These soldiers were ready to invade the island.

But planes from Henderson Field were able to get in the air to attack the transports. With help from army bombers from Espirito Santo Island to the south and planes from the flattop *Enterprise*, seven transports were sunk with the loss of about 10,000 Japanese troops and most of their supplies. On November 14 and 15, nighttime air and sea battles continued with heavy losses to both sides.

A large part of the 38th Japanese Division had been destroyed when the seven transports were sunk. The remaining transports were deliberately run aground on Guadalcanal beaches to unload their cargos. General Vandegrift increased his attacks on the enemy as they tried to come ashore. Lieutenant Colonel Evans F. Carlson's legendary Second Marine Raider Battalion distinguished itself with a long scouting expedition behind enemy lines. His men

A Japanese troop carrier, damaged and unable to launch landing craft at sea, was run ashore on Guadalcanal.

attacked and destroyed many Japanese units after their disastrous landing attempt.

Change of Command

After four months of bitter fighting and heavy losses, victory was in sight for the American forces on Guadalcanal. The marines on the ground, the Cactus Air Force in the air and the U.S. Navy at sea fought together to ensure this victory.

On December 9, 1942, Major General Alexander Patch of the U.S. Army took over command of the Guadalcanal ground forces from General Vandegrift. General Patch brought with him the Army's 25th Infantry Division and the 2nd Marine Division. General Vandegrift and the First Marine Division began withdrawing that same day for a much-deserved rest.

With over 40,000 American troops including fresh reinforcements at his command, General Patch launched his first offensive in mid-December. He immediately captured the high ground at Mount Austen and continued to attack the Japanese on all fronts.

In January the Japanese decided to give up the fight. They immediately started moving troops out and by early February they were all gone. The long and bitter struggle was over. Guadalcanal belonged to the hard-fighting American forces.

After six months of bitter fighting the American casualties on Guadalcanal numbered about 6,000, including more than 1,700 killed or missing in action. Thousands more were suffering from malaria or dengue fever. The U.S. Navy lost some 2,000 sailors and fliers in sea and air battles. The Japanese army and navy casualties were nearly 50,000, with over 29,000 dead.

Marine raider detachments such as this one slipped behind enemy lines to destroy their lines of communication and to attack from the rear.

A Closer Look at . . .

A VICTORIOUS ARMY

The U.S. Army's 25th Division streams ashore to complete the defeat of the Japanese on Guadalcanal.

MOUNTAINS OF SUPPLIES

In January of 1943 the tides of war had turned against the Japanese. American industrial might was producing and delivering the supplies needed to support the rapidly advancing U.S. forces in the South Pacific.

GLOSSARY

ace A pilot who has successfully shot down five enemy aircraft.

aircraft carrier A flat-topped ship on which aircraft take off and land.

Allies The nations that joined together during World War II to defeat Germany, Japan and Italy: France, Great Britain, the Soviet Union and the United States.

anti-aircraft guns Large cannon or machine guns used to shoot at attacking aircraft.

artillery Large weapons such as cannons, howitzers and missile launchers suitably mounted and fired by a crew.

battleship The largest modern warship.

cruiser A high-speed warship, next in size to a battleship.

destroyer A small, high-speed and highly maneuverable naval vessel armed with torpedoes, guns and depth charges.

dive-bomber An aircraft designed to aim and release a bomb at a target while in a nearly vertical dive.

flak Exploding anti-aircraft shells.

flamethrower A device that squirts a stream of flaming fuel toward a target.

flattop An aircraft carrier.

landing craft A flat-bottomed boat designed to carry troops and equipment from a ship to shore.

paratroopers Soldiers trained to jump from aircraft using parachutes.

PT boat Patrol-torpedo boat; a small, high-speed motorboat that is equipped with torpedoes and machine guns.

star shell An artillery shell that explodes in midair, releasing a shower of brightly lighted particles to illuminate a target below.

task force A large military force assigned a specific mission.

torpedo A self-propelled underwater missile that explodes on impact with a target.

torpedo-bomber An aircraft designed to carry bombs and to launch torpedoes.

troopship An ocean transport vessel designed to carry troops.

INDEX

Abe, Admiral Horoaki 35
ace 39, 40, 41
aircraft carrier 7, 9, 14, 30, 32, 33, 34, 36, 38, 39, 42
anti-aircraft fire 32
artillery 18, 21, 25, 26, 40
Astoria 29
Australia 5, 6, 7, 9, 11, 12, 29, 32

battleship 14, 35
Bauer, Lieutenant Colonel Harold W. "Indian Joe" 41
Bloody Ridge 23, 24, 25
bomber 5, 14, 15, 16, 17, 19, 30, 32, 33, 37, 38, 40, 41, 42
Borneo 6
British colonies 5
Burma 5

Cactus Air Force 26, 37, 38, 40, 43
Callaghan, Rear Admiral Daniel J. 35
Canberra 29
Cape Esperance 34
Carl, Lieutenant Marion 40
Carlson, Lieutenant Colonel Evans F. 42
Chicago 29
China 5
Chokai 29
coastwatchers 12, 13, 15
Coral Sea 7, 8, 10, 11
cruiser 14, 17, 28, 29, 30, 32, 33, 34, 35, 36

destroyer 14, 28, 29, 30, 32, 33, 34, 35
disease 20, 25, 44
dive-bomber 7, 22, 32, 38, 39
Doolittle, Lieutenant Colonel Jimmy 5
Dutch colonies 5

Edson, Lieutenant Colonel Merritt A. 23, 24, 25
Elliot 16
Enterprise 14, 32, 33, 34, 36, 39, 42
Espirito Santo Island 42

fighter plane 7, 14, 30, 32, 33, 37, 38, 39, 40
flamethrower 21
Fletcher, Rear Admiral Frank J. 14, 18, 30, 31, 32
Florida Island 11
fortified encampment 17, 18
Foss, Captain Joseph J. 41
French colonies 5

Ghormley, Vice Admiral Robert 10
Goto, Rear Admiral Aritomo 34
Great Britain 5, 12, 13, 15
Guadalcanal air force 37, 38

Hawaii 5, 7, 9, 10
Henderson Field 16, 17, 18, 20, 21, 24, 26, 27, 30, 32, 33, 34, 35, 36, 37, 38, 39, 40, 41, 42
Henderson, Major Loften 16
Hiei 35
Hong Kong 5
Hornet 5, 34, 39
Hyakutake, Lieutenant General Haruyoshi 26, 27

Ichiki, Colonel Kyono 20, 21
Indochina 5
Ironbottom Sound 17, 28, 35

Jarvis 16
Juneau 36

Kawaguchi, Major General Kiyotaje 23, 24

Kincaid, Admiral Thomas C. 34

landing craft 14, 15, 40
leathernecks 15, 19, 27
Lexington 7, 8
Lunga Point 15

MacArthur, General Douglas 5
Malay Peninsula 5
Marine Raiders 15, 42, 44
Matanikau River 25, 26
Medal of Honor 40
Midway 7, 9, 10, 16, 40
Mount Austen 16, 44

New Guinea 7, 10, 11
North Carolina 33

Operation Watchtower 13

Pacific Ocean 5, 6, 7, 9, 10, 12, 36,
    37, 38
Pacific Fleet 5, 7, 10, 28, 36
paratrooper 23, 24, 25
Patch, Major General Alexander
    43
Pearl Harbor 5
Philippine Islands 5, 6
Port Moresby 6, 7, 11
President Coolidge 31
PT boat 36

Quincy 29

reconnaissance 39, 40
Red Beach 15, 16, 18, 20, 28
Ryujo 33

Santa Cruz Islands 34, 39
Saratoga 14, 32
Savo Island 17, 28, 29, 30, 34
Scott, Rear Admiral Norman 34
Sendai Division 26, 27
Shoho 7

Shokaku 7, 32
Skylark Channel 13, 16, 17, 28
slot 11, 12, 17, 22, 28, 34, 35
Smith, Major John L. 40
Solomon Islands 6, 11, 12, 13, 22,
    25, 26, 28, 30, 31, 33, 34, 39
South Pacific 6, 12, 36, 37
Sullivan brothers 36

Tenaru River 21, 25, 27
Thailand 5
Tokyo 5, 6, 23
Tokyo Express 22, 33, 34
Tojo, Japanese Premier Hideki 10
torpedo-bomber 7, 16, 29, 32, 38,
    39
troop transport 13, 28, 30, 31, 32,
    33, 34, 35, 42, 43
Tulagi Island 11, 12, 13, 14, 15,
    18, 23
Turner, Admiral Richard K. 25

U.S. Army 5, 25, 27, 37, 41, 42, 43
U.S. Marine Corps 10, 11, 13, 15,
    16, 17, 18, 19, 20, 21, 22, 23,
    24, 25, 26, 28, 31, 32, 33, 36,
    37, 38, 40, 41, 42, 43, 44, 45
U.S. Navy 6, 7, 10, 22, 25, 28, 29,
    31, 33, 36, 37, 38, 39, 43, 44

Vandegrift, Major General
    Alexander A. 13, 15, 18, 20,
    23, 24, 25, 42, 43
Vincennes 29

Wake Island 6
Wasp 14, 32, 33, 35, 39
World War II 12, 41

Yamamoto, Admiral Isoroku 7, 10
Yorktown 7, 8

Zuikaku 32